LOOKING AFTER YOUR PET

Cat

Text by Clare Hibbert

Photography by Robert and Justine Pickett

HODDER
Wayland

an imprint of Hodder Children's Books

Titles in the LOOKING AFTER YOUR PET series:

Cat • Dog • Hamster • Rabbit
Guinea Pig • Fish

For more information on this series and other Hodder Wayland titles, go to
www.hodderwayland.co.uk

© 2004 White-Thomson Publishing Ltd

Produced by White-Thomson Publishing Ltd
2/3 St Andrew's Place, Lewes, BN7 1UP

Editor: Elaine Fuoco-Lang
Inside design: Leishman Design
Cover design: Hodder Wayland
Photographs: Robert Pickett
Proofreader: Alison Cooper

Published in Great Britain in 2004 by Hodder
Wayland, an imprint of Hodder Children's Books.
This paperback edition published in 2005

Hodder Children's Books
An imprint of Hodder Headline Limited
338 Euston Road, London, NW1 3BH

British Library Cataloguing in Publication Data
Hibbert, Clare
   Cat. - (Looking after your pet)
   1.Cats - Juvenile literature
   I.Title
   636.8'083

ISBN 0 7502 4519 0

Acknowledgements
The publishers would like to thank the following
for their assistance with this book:
The PDSA (Reg. Charity 283483) for their help
and assistance with the series.

The Lord Whisky Sanctuary Fund
(Reg. Charity 283483) for the kittens and
Mrs Margaret Todd, MBE.

Cover picture: Digital Vision/Getty Images

The website addresses (URLs) included in this
book were valid at the time of going to press.
However, because of the nature of the Internet,
it is possible that some addresses may have
changed, or sites may have changed or closed
down since publication. While the author,
packager and publisher regret any inconvenience
that this may cause readers, no responsibility for
any such changes can be accepted by either the
author, the packager or the publisher.

Printed in China

Contents

Choosing a cat

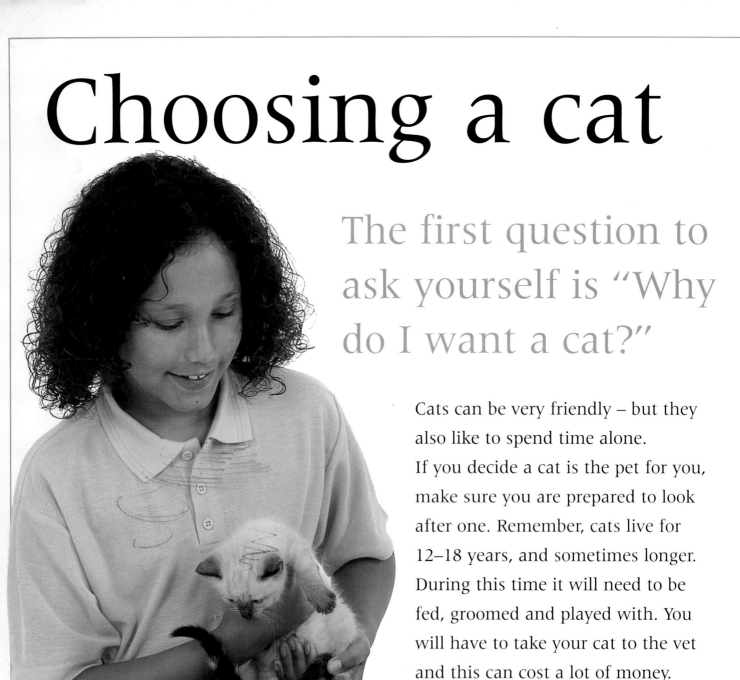

The first question to ask yourself is "Why do I want a cat?"

Cats can be very friendly – but they also like to spend time alone. If you decide a cat is the pet for you, make sure you are prepared to look after one. Remember, cats live for 12–18 years, and sometimes longer. During this time it will need to be fed, groomed and played with. You will have to take your cat to the vet and this can cost a lot of money.

◀ Most of us want a cat as a companion and do not mind whether it is a special breed or a moggy.

You will find adverts for kittens in your local paper. You could also take on a cat from a rescue centre.

▼ Ask to see your kitten with its mother. What she's like is a good clue to your kitten's personality.

Top Tips

Choosing a cat checklist

🐾 Is the cat healthy? Look for bright eyes, clean ears and soft fur without tiny black specks left by fleas.

🐾 Cat or kitten? A kitten is adorable but will need a lot more care.

🐾 Cats, like people, have personalities. Choose a cat that seems playful and confident.

A home for your cat

Cats, like all animals, need warmth and shelter, food and water, rest and exercise.

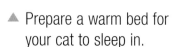

▲ Prepare a warm bed for your cat to sleep in.

A new cat, especially a kitten, needs plenty of attention. Keep it in one room at first, until it has settled in. Place a blanket in a basket or box to make a cosy bed. Put out food and water bowls. You will also need a litter tray for your cat to use whenever it is not allowed outside. Keep new cats inside for one to two weeks. Kittens should not go out until a vet has given them all their jabs (see page 23).

Checklist: cat kit

- Food
- Grooming brush
- Carrying case
- Cat flap
- Scratching post

- Food and water bowl

Find toys for your cat. They love to hide in boxes or pounce on balls of wool or paper. Empty toilet rolls are entertaining, too. Play helps cats to develop good reactions.

▶ Cats scratch to keep their claws in good condition. To keep your furniture scratch-free, buy a scratching post.

• Litter tray and cat litter

• Toys

• Cat bed

Caring for kittens

Just like human babies, kittens need extra-special care.

▲ Kittens can be mischievous. Make sure you are firm with them so they don't develop bad habits.

▼ Train your kitten to use a litter tray. Make the tray smell right by adding dirty litter taken from the kitten's old tray.

Give your kitten lots of cuddles and strokes. Say your kitten's name as much as possible. Soon your kitten will know the sound of its name and come when you call.

Its mother will have given the kitten some toilet training but you must teach it to use its new litter tray. If your kitten goes to the toilet in the wrong place, clean the area thoroughly with a biological cleaner so no smell lingers. If the kitten keeps going there, try blocking off the area with sheets of kitchen foil or piles of coat hangers – cats hate both these things!

Make sure your kitten is used to being with people. Don't let it grow up with bad habits. Its bite might not hurt now, but this will be different when the kitten becomes an adult! When your kitten is naughty, move it away and say 'No!' firmly.

Pet Talk

How soon can I take a kitten home?

Cats are mammals like us, which means that the mothers feed their babies on milk. A kitten should not be taken away from its mother until it has stopped suckling and is eating solid foods. This is called weaning. It happens when the kitten is eight to ten weeks old.

▼ Once the kitten is old enough to be taken home you should make sure you know how to hold it properly. You must support the whole of the kitten's body and make sure you don't grip too tightly or you could hurt it.

Life outside

Your cat wants to explore the outside world.

Do you have a garden, or somewhere safe where your cat can be outside? Fit a cat flap so your cat can come and go as it pleases.

▼ Your cat will love exploring the garden – especially if there is a tree that it can climb.

◀ Encourage your cat to use a cat flap. Your cat will soon become used to it and be able to go in and out as it wishes.

Your cat will have secret places where it takes outdoor naps. But it also has many places it visits each day.

Have you ever noticed the way your cat rubs at things? It is using special scent glands to leave behind a smell marker. This message to other cats says "I have been here! This place is mine!" Every cat has its own territory.

Pet Talk
What is neutering?

It is best to have your cat neutered. A vet will do this when your cat is around five months old. Neutering stops females becoming pregnant. Neutering a male cat will stop it from picking fights, racing after females and spraying urine inside your house to mark its territory.

▶ Male cats that have not been neutered are called toms. They are not ideal house pets. Tomcats spray smelly urine to mark their territory – and they will do this inside the house, not just outdoors.

Feeding your cat

Just like you,
a cat needs to
eat healthy
foods.

Cats are carnivores or meat-
eaters. They need to eat meat
and fish to stay healthy.
An adult cat needs two meals
a day. You can feed cats fresh
food or buy special cat food.
There are two main types,
wet or dry. A diet of only
tinned, wet food is bad
for your cat's teeth.

▶ Your kitten should eat up to
five small meals a day.

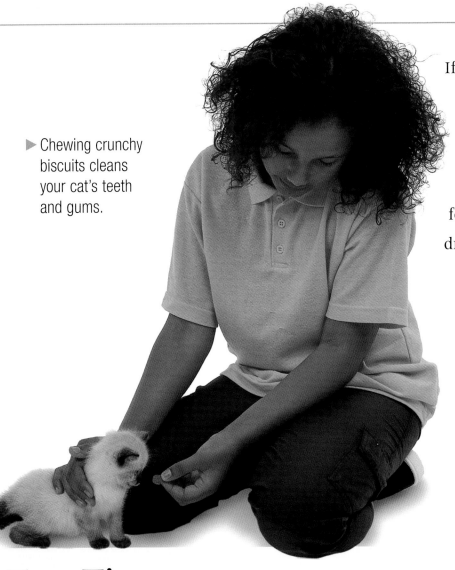

▶ Chewing crunchy biscuits cleans your cat's teeth and gums.

If your cat is eating tinned food, give it crunchy treats or even an occasional chunk of boneless chicken. A diet of only dry biscuits can be bad for your cat, too, unless it drinks plenty of water.

▼ Not all cats like milk but if your cat does, don't give it too much. Cow's milk can cause tummy upsets.

Top Tips
Cat food

🐾 Remove bones from cooked fish and chicken.

🐾 Cats over six months old need two meals a day.

🐾 Feed kittens on special kitten food.

🐾 Don't try to make your cat a vegetarian. It needs meat.

🐾 Some cats don't like the chemicals in tap water. Try clean bottled still water.

🐾 Don't overfeed your cat.

Everyday care

It's your job to keep an eye on your cat's health.

Make time every day to have a long cuddle with your cat. While you stroke your cat check for bumps, especially along the tail. These could be bites and sometimes they can become infected.

◀ Get to know your cat so you can check its health each day.

Also, check that your cat's eyes are bright and clear. 'Sleep' in the eyes may mean an eye infection if there's lots of it. Check, too, that your cat's ears are clean, and not waxy. Also make sure that its claws are not split or torn. If you spot any of these signs of illness, you will need to take your cat to see a vet.

▲ This cat is scratching a tree to keep its claws short.

Pet Talk
Claw care

Most cats do not need their claws clipped. Walking on patios and scratching trees stops claws growing too long. And don't forget, your cat needs claws to climb – and they are its best defence in a fight. If claws really do need cutting, use clippers designed for cats, not nail scissors. Ask an adult to do this or, better still, your vet.

◀ This cat is bright and alert so you can tell it has been well cared for by its owner.

Grooming

Your cat likes to keep itself spotlessly clean.

You need to help your cat to groom. A long-haired cat cannot keep its fur in good condition all by itself. It needs you to brush and comb it at least once a day. A short-haired cat needs brushing only when it is moulting, or losing its fur, which happens about twice a year. But it is still a good idea to comb its fur regularly. This keeps your cat used to being groomed and allows you to check for fleas, too.

▲ The cat's body is so bendy that its tongue can reach every bit of it – almost! For the top of the head, your cat relies on a licked paw instead.

▶ Cats are always cleaning themselves, but you should still groom your cat with a brush to make sure its coat stays sleek.

Pet Talk

Hair balls

If you do not groom your cat, it will swallow loose hair. This can get stuck in its throat and form hard hair balls. Cats try to stop the hair balls tickling their throat by eating grass. Grass makes them vomit and they throw up the loose hair.

▶ Be gentle when you groom your cat. Soon it will relax and enjoy it!

17

Enjoying your cat

Learn to listen when your cat talks to you!

Your cat tells you how it is feeling by the noises it makes. A miaow means it wants something. You'll soon know if this means food, games or a cuddle. A purr shows that your cat feels cosy and content. Listen out for the chirrup – your cat is saying "hello"!

◄ Watch your kitten's body language as it plays. You can tell when your kitten is alert, because its ears and whiskers twitch.

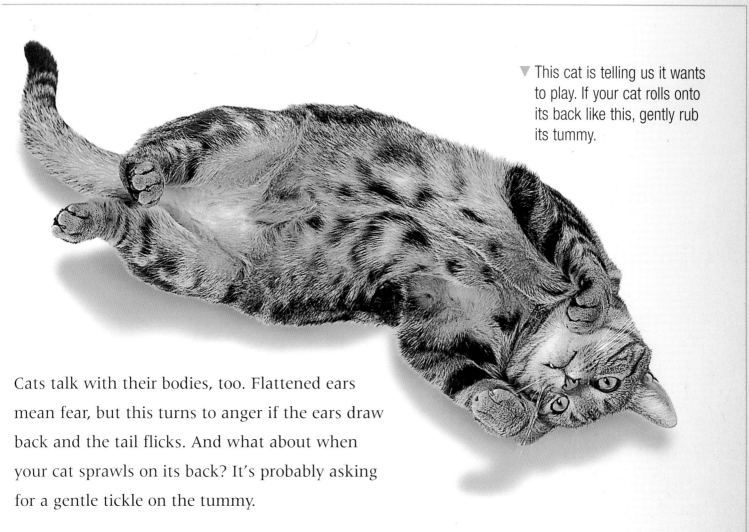

▼ This cat is telling us it wants to play. If your cat rolls onto its back like this, gently rub its tummy.

Cats talk with their bodies, too. Flattened ears mean fear, but this turns to anger if the ears draw back and the tail flicks. And what about when your cat sprawls on its back? It's probably asking for a gentle tickle on the tummy.

▶ See how this cat's eyes are half-closed? Wide-eyed staring is a sign of aggression or fear.

Top Tips
Cat manners

🐾 Staring is rude! Half-close your eyelids so your cat doesn't feel threatened.

🐾 Want to make friends with a cat? Look in the other direction but stretch out your hand to be sniffed.

🐾 Check that younger brothers or sisters are gentle with your pet. It is a living animal, not a toy.

Cats will be cats

Are you ready to live with a hunter?

It's thousands of years since the first wild cats became tame enough to live with people. But your pet is sure to have kept a wild streak! Most cats like to stalk small animals and will bring you their catch. Be prepared for mice, birds, frogs – even your neighbour's goldfish. If the creature is not badly harmed, put it back outside.

▼ This cat has caught a rat. It might be taking it to its owner as a present!

Try not to get too upset about this side of your cat's nature. Hunting is an important part of being a cat. Even the games you enjoy with your cat are practice for hunting.

◀ However well-fed your cat, it will probably hunt. This cat is hunting a bird. Cats rarely eat their catch.

▶ It is fine to attract birds to your garden. Just make sure your bird table is cat-proof! This pole is too slippery for a cat to climb.

Top Tips
Saving wildlife

🐾 A mesh covering protects pond creatures from cats – and hungry herons, too.

🐾 Place bird tables, baths and nesting boxes out of reach of cats.

🐾 An elastic collar with a bell or a quick release collar will warn wildlife, but could be dangerous to your cat (see page 22).

Taking care

Sometimes, cats go missing for several days or more.

Be prepared for this. Ask your vet to microchip your cat. The tiny chip goes under the cat's skin but don't worry, your cat won't feel a thing. It contains information such as your name and address. You could also give your cat a collar, but this can catch on trees or railings. If you want your cat to wear one, make sure it is a quick release collar or made from safety elastic.

◀ You must take responsibility for your cat. This cat has been microchipped. The vet is scanning the chip to read the owner's details.

Getting lost is not the only danger your cat faces in the outside world. Your vet will advise you about jabs to protect your cat from disease.

Don't allow your kitten out until it has had its jabs and remember that most jabs need top-up boosters every year or two. Keep careful records so you know your cat is fully protected.

Checklist: which jabs?

Don't worry about the long names. Just make sure your pel is protected against the three main killer diseases:

- Feline infectious enteritis
- Feline infectious respiratory disease (Cat flu)
- Feline leukaemia

▶ Vets usually inject cats at the back of the neck. Cats don't have many nerves here, so they are less likely to feel pain.

A trip to the vet

Even the most cared-for cats may get hurt or ill.

An injury is not always easy to spot – but if your cat won't stop licking a certain area, it is probably hurt. Signs of illness include runny eyes or nose, an upset tummy or lack of appetite. If you are worried, ring your vet for an appointment.

◀ Your vet may put your cat in a collar like this. It will stop your pet licking at sores or biting at stitches.

Your vet may give you medicine so you can treat your cat at home. You might be nervous when you give your cat its medicine, but be brave and firm with your cat.

Top Tips

Medicine for cats

🐾 Give no more than the correct dose – and only to the pet named on the label.

🐾 Never give human medicine to your cat.

🐾 With tablets, hold the mouth open, place far back on the tongue, then close the mouth. Stroke your cat's throat until it swallows.

🐾 With eye drops, hold the head back until the eye is totally covered.

🐾 With ear drops, rub behind the ear so the drops trickle down deep.

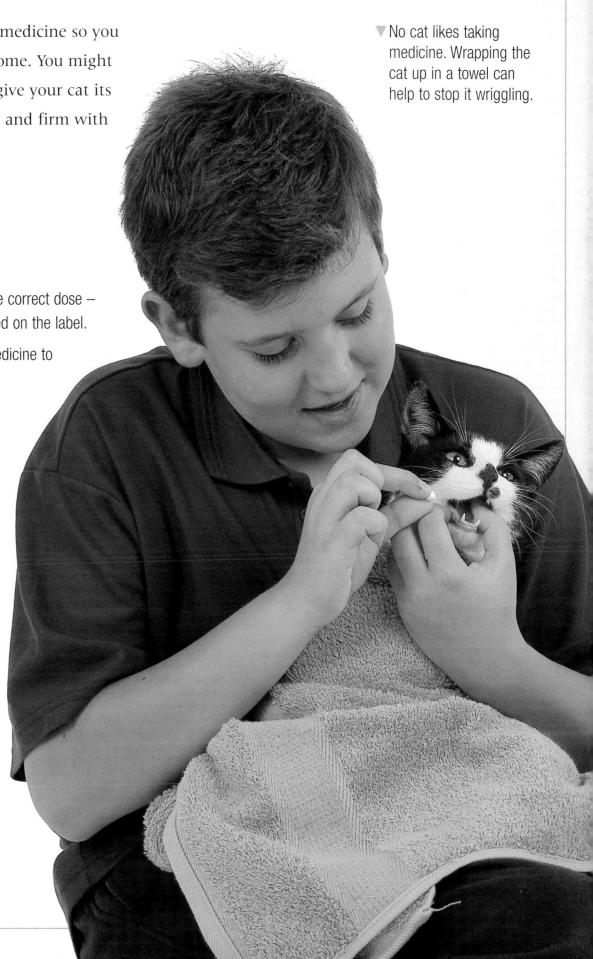

▼ No cat likes taking medicine. Wrapping the cat up in a towel can help to stop it wriggling.

Holiday time

Don't forget about your cat when you go on holiday!

▲ Always place your cat safely in its carrying case when travelling. Never let a cat loose inside the car.

You could take your cat with you, but most cats hate being in strange, new places. Yours might try to run away. Cats can get travel sick, too.

The best option is to ask a friend or neighbour to visit your house twice a day to feed and check on your pet. Remember to give them your vet's telephone number just in case. Your cat may miss you, but at least it is in its own territory.

◀ Cats are happiest on home turf, where there are no strange noises or smells to worry them.

If this is not possible, book your cat into a good cattery. Visit beforehand to check that the cats there are clean and well cared for.

Checklist: choosing a cattery

- Is the place clean?
- Will your cat have its own cabin?
- Is there a cosy sleeping area?
- Is there space to play and climb?
- Did the cattery ask to see proof that your cat has had its jabs?

If not, don't go there!

▶ Never leave your cat to look after itself. Book it into a cattery if no one can go to feed your pet.

Cat facts

Did you know that the ancient Egyptians kept the first pet cats? Read on for more fun facts.

- The ancient Egyptians also worshipped a cat goddess!

- In the UK, people say that black cats bring good luck. But in the USA, black cats are unlucky!

- Cats have baby teeth just like you! They start to fall out when the cat is about 14 weeks old.

- A cat spends 70 per cent of its time sleeping – that's double the amount of sleep that you get.

- The Manx is a breed of cat that has no tail.

- The first ever cat show was held in London in 1871.

- Would you like a cat with curly hair? Try a Cornish Rex or an American Wirehair.

- A cat's sense of smell is 30 times better than yours – but you have 18 times more taste buds than a cat.

- Cats have five toes on each front paw, but only four toes on each back paw.

- All-white cats with blue eyes are nearly always deaf.

- Cats have litters of between one and ten kittens. But the largest litter on record was 14 Persian kittens born in South Africa in 1974.

- Kittens are born with their eyes closed. When they first open, they are always blue.

- The oldest pet cat on record was Granpa Rex. He lived to be 34 years old.

Glossary

Breed
A particular type of cat, such as a Persian or a Siamese.

Carnivore
A meat-eater.

Cat flap
A door that allows your cat to go outside – and come back in again.

Cat litter
Material that is put inside a litter tray.

Feline infectious enteritis
A virus that kills cats. There is no cure, but you can protect against it with a jab. Symptoms include stomach cramps and vomiting.

Feline infectious respiratory disease (cat flu)
A viral disease that can kill cats if not treated quickly, but you can protect against it with a jab. Symptoms include sneezing, running eyes and nose, and drooling.

Feline leukaemia
A virus that kills more cats than any other infectious disease, but you can protect against it with a jab. Symptoms include tumours, gum disease and kidney failure.

Fleas
Insect pests that live on cats. Ask your vet for advice on how to get rid of fleas. You will need to treat your home to get rid of any flea eggs, too.

Grooming
Cleaning a cat's fur. This is partly done by the cat with its tongue, and partly done by you with a brush or a comb.

Hair balls
Pellets of hair that can clog up a cat's throat. Grooming your cat regularly should prevent hair balls.

Jabs
Injections that protect against serious disease.

Litter tray
A shallow container that is filled with cat litter. This is where your cat goes to the toilet and it should be cleaned out fully at least once a week. Shy cats might prefer a litter tray with a lid.

Microchip
A tiny computer chip, the size of a grain of rice. This is placed under the skin of your cat and contains information about you, the owner. This can be read by special scanners if your cat is ever lost.

Moggy
An ordinary cat that does not belong to a particular breed.

Moulting
Losing fur. Long-haired cats moult all year round. Short-haired cats moult twice a year – at the beginning of summer when they lose their thicker, winter coat, and at the beginning of winter when they lose their thinner, summer coat.

Neutering
Removing a cat's sex organs. This stops females from getting pregnant and makes males less likely to get into fights.

Rescue centre
A place that looks after lost or abandoned animals.

Scent glands
Places on a cat's skin that produce a smell. Cats have scent glands on the cheeks, above the eyes, and at the root of the tail.

Territory
The area of land that belongs to your cat! For most neutered cats, their territory is just their owner's garden. Tomcats have much larger territories.

Tomcat
A male cat that has not been neutered.

Vegetarian
Does not eat meat or fish.

Vet
An animal doctor.

Weaning
Moving a kitten on to solid foods, away from mother's milk.

Further information

Books

My Pet: Kitten by Honor Head, photographs by Jane Burton
(Belitha Press, 2002)

Cats by Michaela Miller
(Heinemann Library, 1998)

The Best-Ever Book of Cats by Amanda O'Neill
(Kingfisher Books, 1998)

Looking After Your Pet Cat by Helen Piers
(Frances Lincoln, 2002)

Kitten to Cat by Jillian Powell
(Hodder Wayland, 2001)

Useful Addresses

PDSA
Whitechapel Way
Priorslee
Telford
Shropshire
TF2 9PQ
Tel: 01952 290999
Fax: 01952 291035
Website: www.pdsa.org.uk

RSPCA
Wilberforce Way
Southwater
Horsham
West Sussex
RH13 9RS
Tel: 0870 3335 999
Fax: 0870 7530 284
Website: www.rspca.org.uk

Index